HAL•LEONARD®

DRUM PLAY-ALONG

VOL. 41

AUDIO ACCESS INCLUDED

PLAYBACK+
Speed • Pitch • Balance • Loop

Rock SONGS FOR KIDS

Play 8 Songs with Sound-Alike Audio

To access audio visit:
www.halleonard.com/mylibrary

Enter Code
5475-9302-5592-9023

ISBN 978-1-4950-2836-6

7777 W. Bluemound Rd. P.O. Box 13819 Milwaukee, WI 53213

For all works contained herein:
Unauthorized copying, arranging, adapting, recording, Internet posting, public performance, or other distribution of the printed or recorded music in this publication is an infringement of copyright. Infringers are liable under the law.

Visit Hal Leonard Online at
www.halleonard.com

Rock SONGS FOR KIDS

Play 8 Songs with Sound-Alike Audio

CONTENTS

Page	Title
4	ABC THE JACKSON 5
12	Happy PHARRELL
9	I Love Rock 'N Roll JOAN JETT & THE BLACKHEARTS
16	I'm a Believer THE MONKEES
21	Let's Get It Started BLACK EYED PEAS
32	Low Rider WAR
28	Surfin' U.S.A. THE BEACH BOYS
37	Yellow Submarine THE BEATLES

ABC

Words and Music by Alphonso Mizell, Frederick Perren,
Deke Richards and Berry Gordy

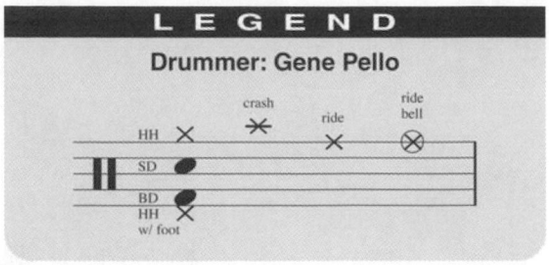

Intro

Moderately ♩ = 94

Ba, bum, bum, bum, ba, boo. (Da, da, da, da, da, da.) 1. You

𝄋 **Verse**

2nd time, substitute Fill 1

went to school to learn, girl, things you nev-er, nev-er knew be-fore. Li - hi - ike "I"
2. *See additional lyrics*

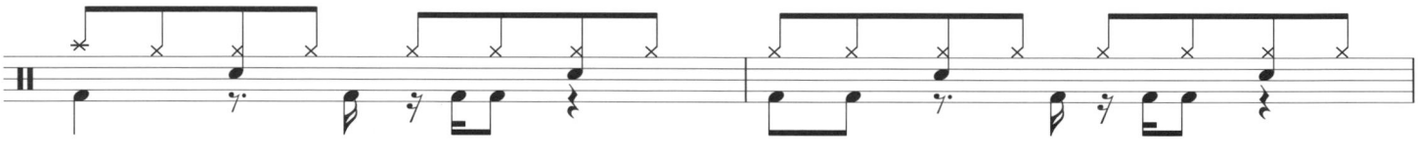

2nd time, substitute Fill 2

be-fore "E" ex-cept af - ter "C" and why two plus two makes four. Now, now, now, I'm

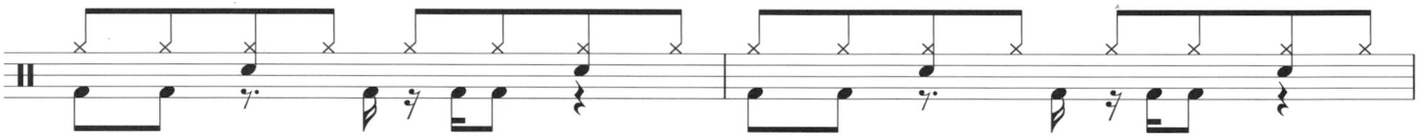

gon-na teach you all a-bout love, dear. Sit

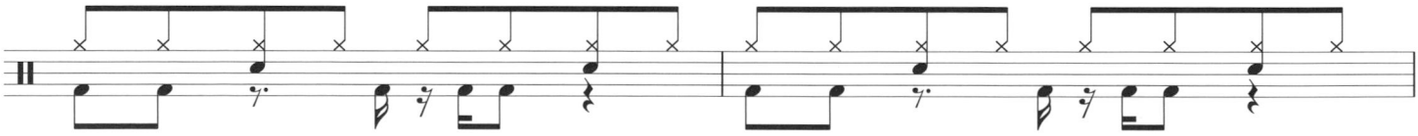

Fill 1

Fill 2

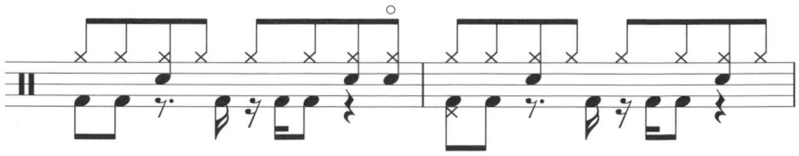

Copyright © 1970 Jobete Music Co., Inc.
Copyright Renewed
All Rights Administered by Sony/ATV Music Publishing LLC, 424 Church Street, Suite 1200, Nashville, TN 37219
International Copyright Secured All Rights Reserved

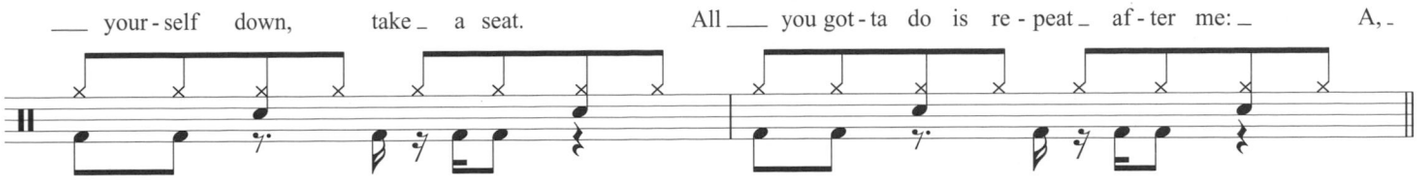

Chorus

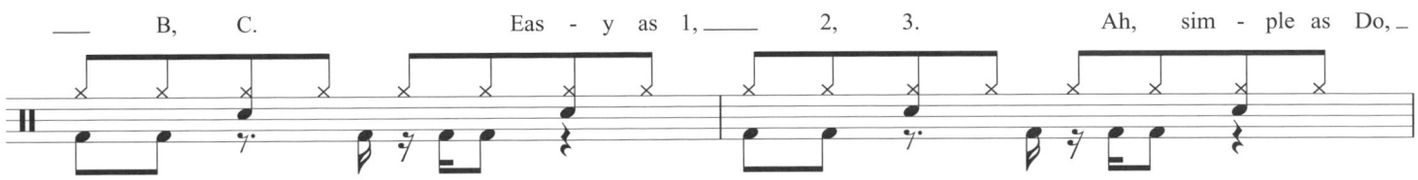

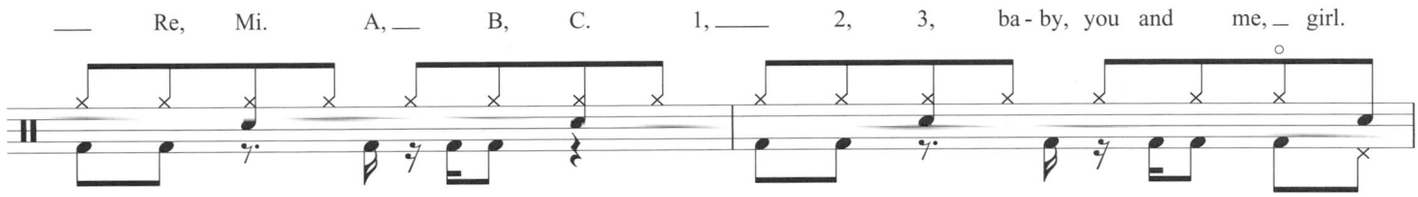

To Coda ⊕

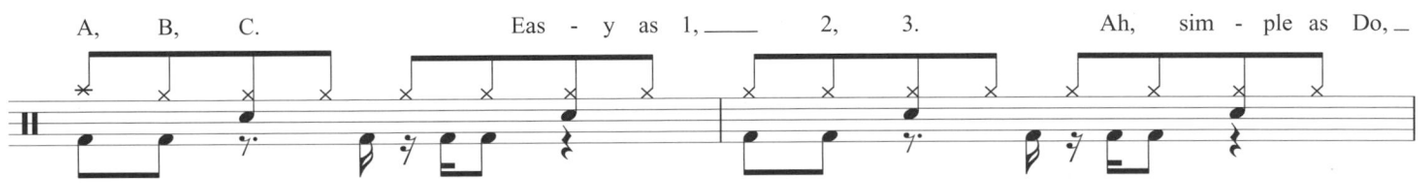

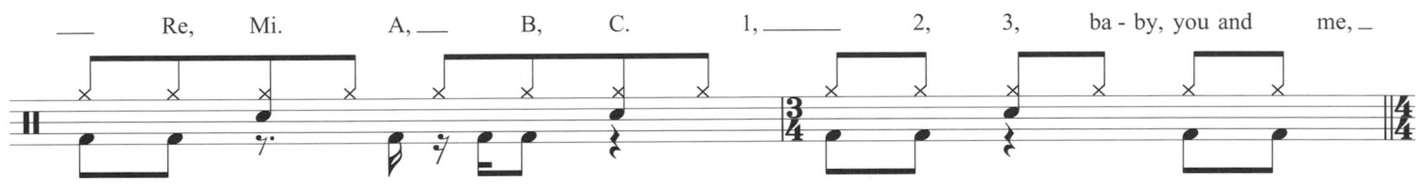

Interlude

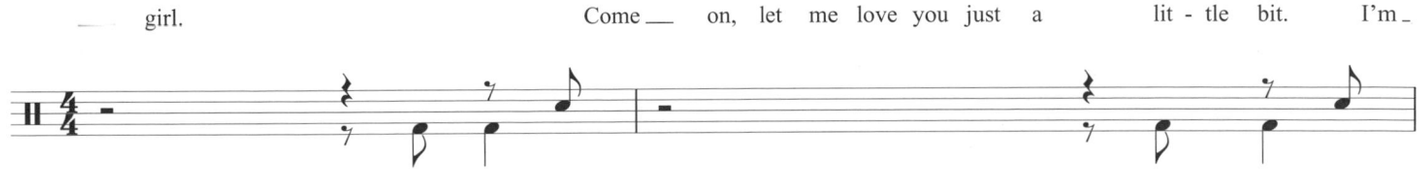

D.S. al Coda

Coda
Re, Mi. A, B, C. That's how eas - y love can be. Now,
that's how eas - y love can be. Sing a sim - ple mel - o - dy. 1,
Bridge
2, 3. You and me!
Sit down, girl!
I think I love you.
No!
Get up, girl!
Show me what you can do.
Shake it, shake it, ba - by. Come on, now.

Outro-Chorus

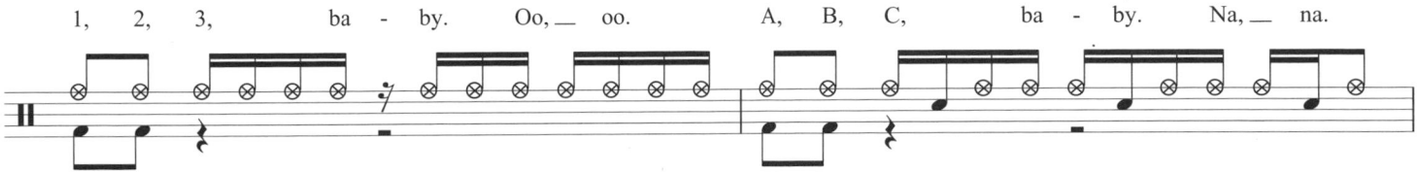

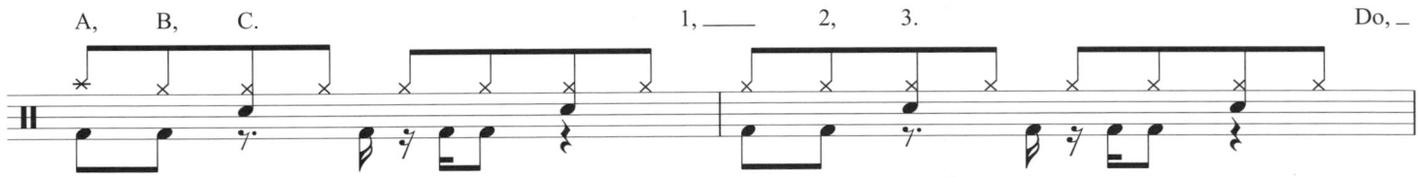

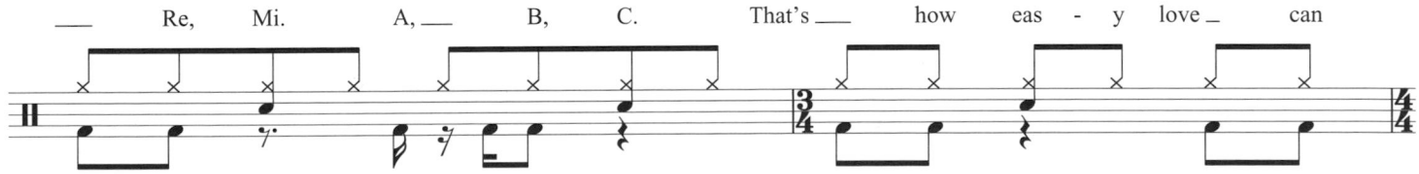

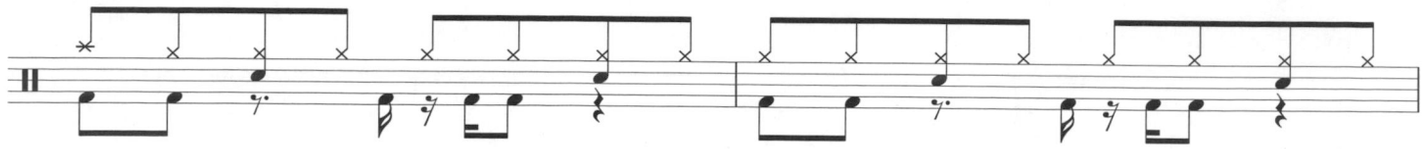

Begin fade

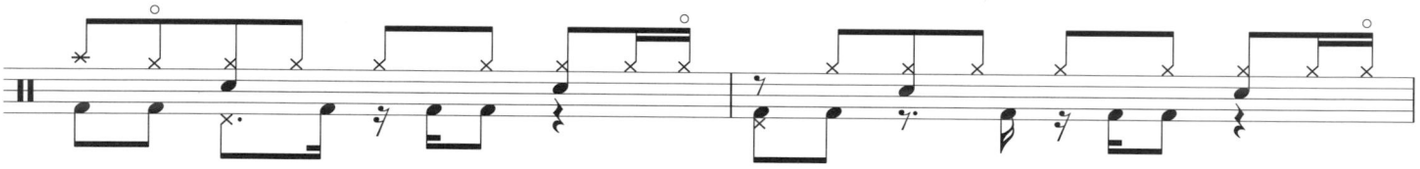

Fade out

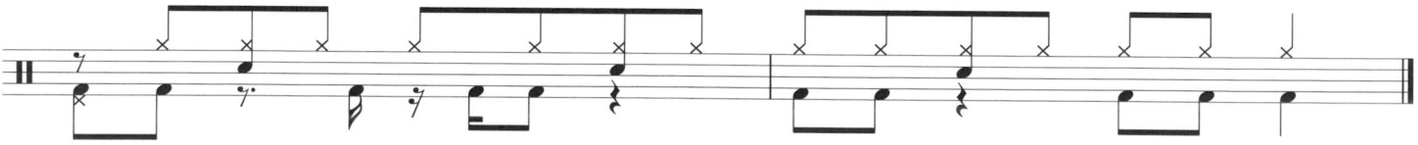

Additional Lyrics

2. Reading and writing, arithmetic,
   Are the branches on the learning tree.
   But listen, without the roots of love ev'ryday, girl,
   Your education ain't complete.
   Te-Te-Te-Teacher's gonna show you how to get an "A".
   Spell "Me", "You"; add the two.
   Listen to me, baby. That's all you gotta do.

I Love Rock 'N Roll

Words and Music by Alan Merrill and Jake Hooker

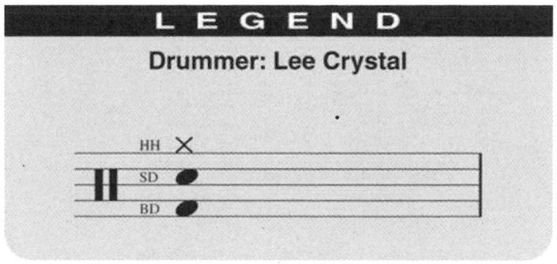

Intro

Moderately slow Rock ♩ = 96

Verse

1. I saw him danc-in' there by the re-cord ma-chine. I
2. *See additional lyrics*

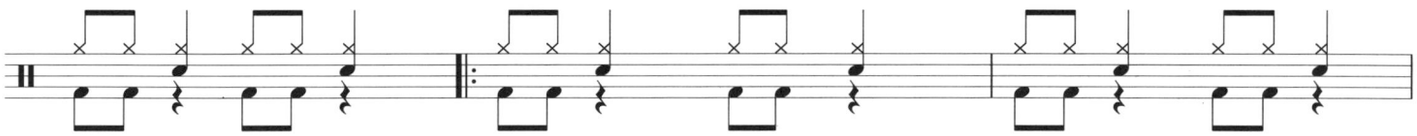

knew he must have been a-bout sev-en-teen. The beat was go-in' strong,

play-in' my fa-vor-ite song. And I could tell it would-n't be long 'til he was with

me, yeah, me! And I could tell it would-n't be long 'til he was with me, yeah, me, sing-in',

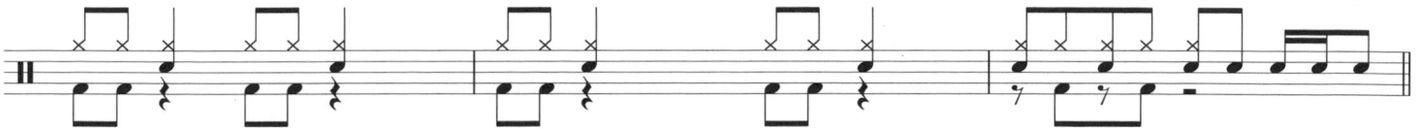

Copyright © 1975, 1982 Rak Publishing Ltd. for the World
Copyright Renewed 2003
All Rights for the U.S.A. and Canada Administered by Kobalt Songs Music Publishing
International Copyright Secured All Rights Reserved

Chorus
I love rock 'n' roll, so put an - oth - er dime in the juke - box, ba - by.
I love rock 'n' roll, so come and take your time and dance with
1.
2nd time, substitute Fill 1
me.
Ow!
2. He
2.
Guitar Solo/Pre-Chorus
Said, "Can I take ya home where
we can be a - lone?"
Next, we were mov - in' on, he was with
Fill 1

Chorus

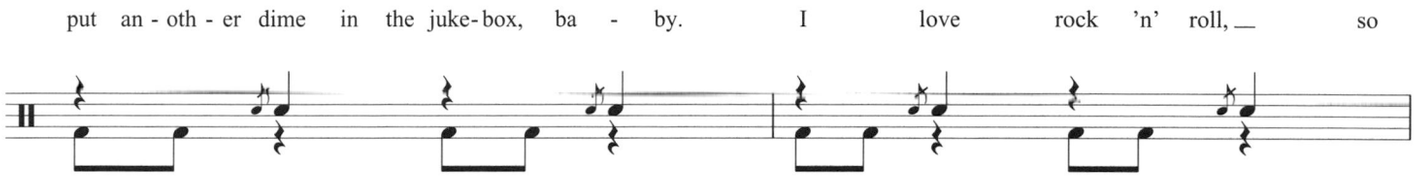

Outro-Chorus

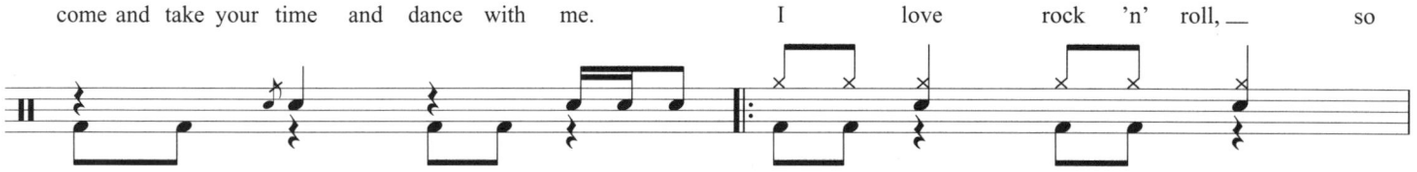

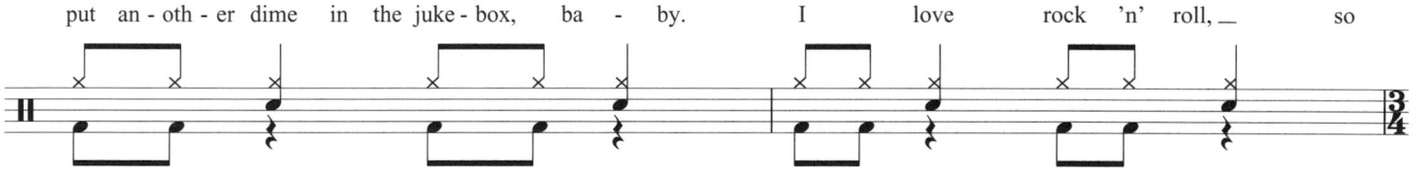

Additional Lyrics

2. He smiled, so I got up and asked for his name.
"That don't matter," he said, "'cause it's all the same."
I said, "Can I take ya home where we can be alone?"
And next, we were movin' on, he was with me, yeah, me!
Next, we were movin' on, he was with me, yeah, me, singin',...

Happy

from DESPICABLE ME 2

Words and Music by Pharrell Williams

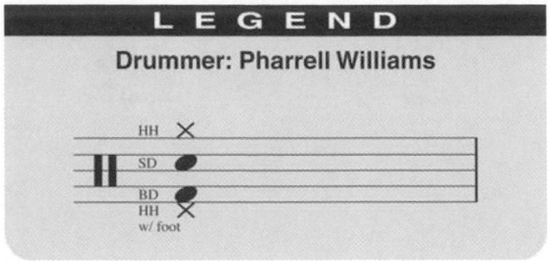

Intro

Moderately fast ♩ = 160

Verse

1. It might seem cra - zy what I'm 'bout to say.
2. *See additional lyrics*

Sun - shine, she's here;

you can take a break. I'm a

hot air bal - loon that could go to space.

With the air, like I don't care, ba - by, by the way.

Copyright © 2013 EMI April Music Inc., More Water From Nazareth and Universal Pictures Music
All Rights on behalf of EMI April Music Inc. and More Water From Nazareth Administered by Sony/ATV Music Publishing LLC,
424 Church Street, Suite 1200, Nashville, TN 37219
All Rights on behalf of Universal Pictures Music Controlled and Administered by Universal Music Corp.
International Copyright Secured All Rights Reserved

Bridge

Bring me down, can't noth-in' bring me down, your love is too high — to bring me down, — can't noth- in' bring me down, — I said.

Bring me down, — can't noth- in' bring me down, — your love is too

high — to bring me down, — can't noth- in' bring me down, — I said. (Be-cause I'm

Chorus

hap - py.) Clap a - long if — you feel — like a room with - out a roof. —

— (Be-cause I'm hap - py.) Clap a - long if — you feel — like

hap - pi - ness is the truth. — (Be - cause I'm hap - py.) Clap a - long — if —

— you know — what hap - pi - ness is to you. — (Be - cause I'm

hap - py.) Clap a - long if — you feel — like that's what you wan - na do. —

Additional Lyrics

2. Here come bad news, talkin' this and that.
Well, gimme all you got and don't hold it back.
Well, I should prob'ly warn you, I'll be just fine.
No offense to you, don't waste your time. Here's why:

I'm a Believer

Words and Music by Neil Diamond

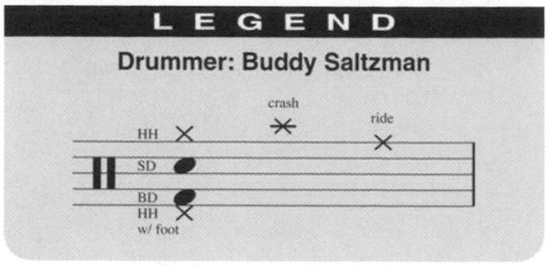

Intro

Moderately fast ♩ = 160

Verse

1. I thought love was on - ly true in fair - y tales,

meant for some-one else but not for me.

Pre-Chorus

Love was out to get me. That's the way it seemed.

Copyright © 1966 TALLYRAND MUSIC, INC. and FORAY MUSIC
Copyright Renewed
All Rights for TALLYRAND MUSIC, INC. Administered by UNIVERSAL TUNES, A Division of SONGS OF UNIVERSAL, INC.
All Rights Reserved Used by Permission

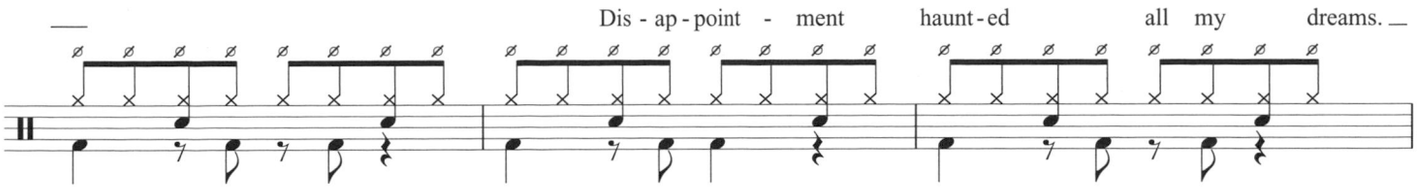

𝄋 Chorus

2nd time, substitute Fill 1
3rd time, substitute Fill 2

To Coda 2 ⊕

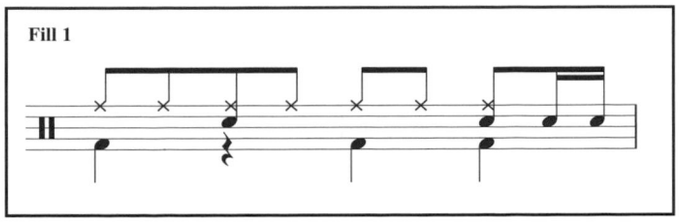

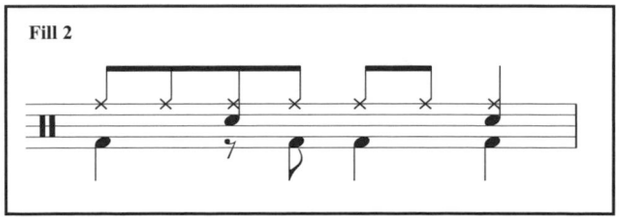

To Coda 1
Verse
2. I thought love was more or less a
giv - in' thing.
Seems the more I gave,
the less I got.
Pre-Chorus
What's the use in try - in'?
All you get is pain.
When I need - ed sun - shine, I got rain.
D.S. al Coda 1
Then I saw her face;

Coda 1

Keyboard Solo

Pre-Chorus

D.S. al Coda 2

Coda 2
Yes, I saw her face; now I'm a be - liev -
- er! Well, not a trace
of doubt in my mind.
Said I'm a be - liev - er, yeah, yeah, yeah, yeah, yeah, yeah.
Begin fade
Said I'm a be - liev - er, yeah.
Fade out
I said I'm a be - liev - er, yeah, yeah, oh.

Let's Get It Started

Words and Music by Will Adams, Allan Pineda, Jaime Gomez,
Michael Fratantuno, George Pajon Jr. and Terence Yoshiaki Graves

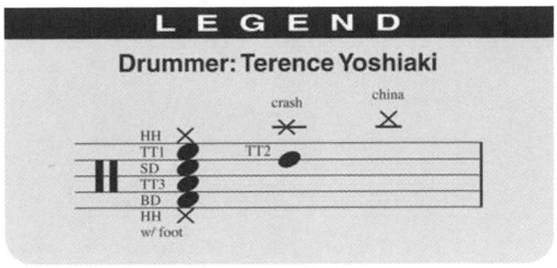

Intro
Moderately ♩ = 105

And the bass keeps run - nin', run - nin' and run - nin', run - nin' and

run - nin', run - nin' and run - nin', run - nin' and run - nin', run - nin' and run - nin', run - nin' and

Verse

run- nin', run - nin' and run- nin', run - nin' and... 1. In this con - text there's no dis - re - spect,

so when I bust my rhymes, you break your necks. We've got five min - utes for us to dis - con - nect

from all in - tel - lect and let the rhy - thm af - fect. To lose the in - hi - bi - tion, fol - low your in - tu - i - tion.

Copyright © 2004 BMG Sapphire Songs (BMI), I Am Composing LLC (BMI), Nawasha Networks Publishing (BMI), BMG Platinum Songs (BMI),
apl de ap publishing LLC (BMI), Tuono Music (BMI), El Cubano Music (BMI) and Hisako Songs (BMI)
Worldwide Rights for BMG Sapphire Songs, I Am Composing LLC, Nawasha Networks Publishing, BMG Platinum Songs and apl de ap Publishing LLC
Administered by BMG Rights Management (US) LLC
All Rights for El Cubano Music Controlled and Administered by EMI Blackwood Music Inc.
International Copyright Secured All Rights Reserved

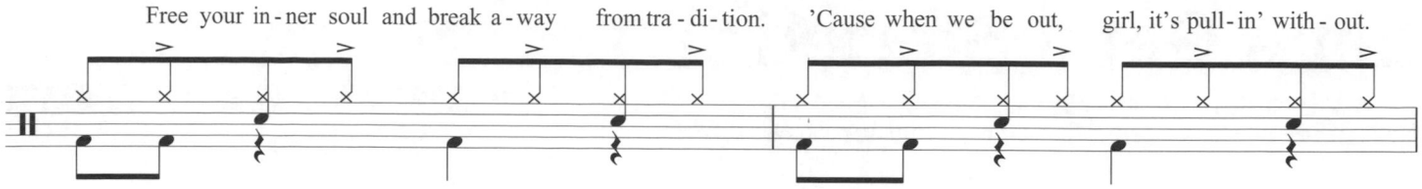

Pre-Chorus

Chorus

Verse

2. Lose _ con - trol of bod - y and soul, don't move _ too fast, peo - ple, just take _ it slow.

Don't get a - head, just jump _ in - to it. Y'all hear _ a - bout it, the Peas - 'll do it.

Get _ start - ed, get __ stu - pid, don't wor - ry 'bout it, peo - ple, we'll walk you through it.

Step by step, like a in - fant, new _ kid. Inch by inch, with the new so - lu - tion.

Trans - mit hits with no de - lu - sion, the feel - ing's ir - re - sist - i - ble and that's how we move _ it.

Pre-Chorus

Ev - 'ry - bod - y, ev - 'ry - bod - y just get __ in - to it and get __ stu -

pid. Get it start - ed, get it start - ed, get it start - ed. Let's get it

Chorus

Interlude

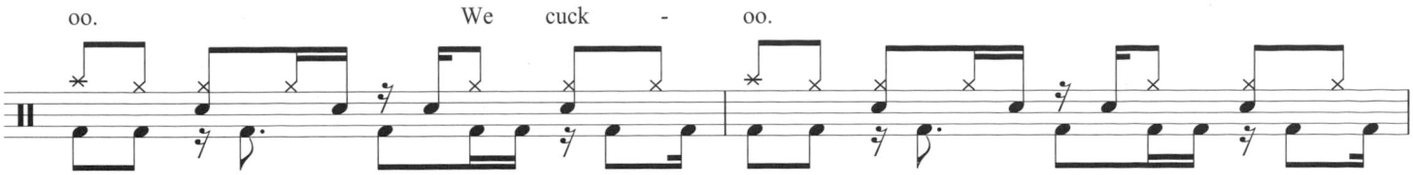
oo. We cuck - oo.

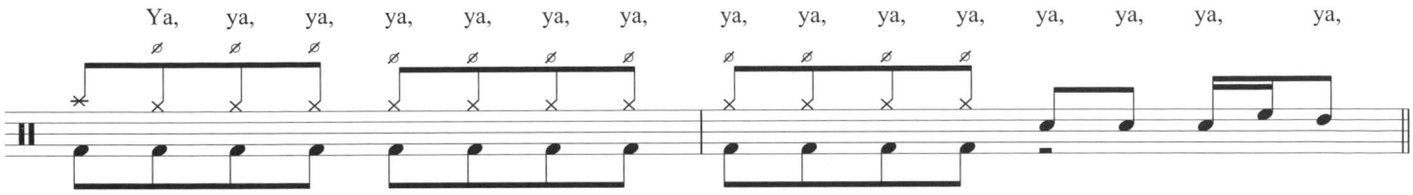
Ya, ya, ya, ya, ya, ya, ya, ya, ya, ya, ya, ya, ya, ya, ya,

Bridge

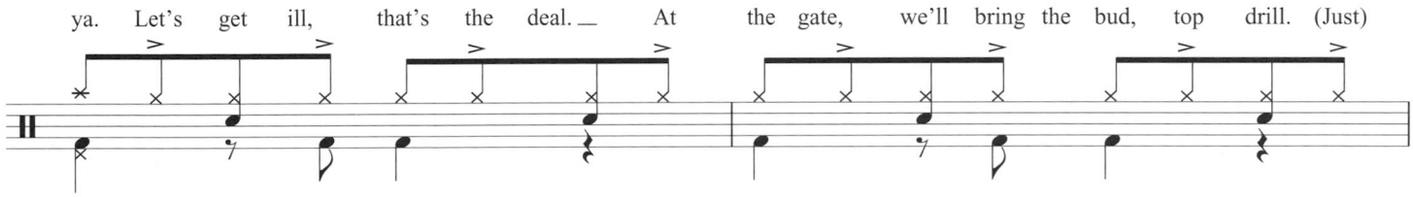
ya. Let's get ill, that's the deal. At the gate, we'll bring the bud, top drill. (Just)

lose your mind, this is the time, y'all guessed this ill just to bang your spine. (Just)

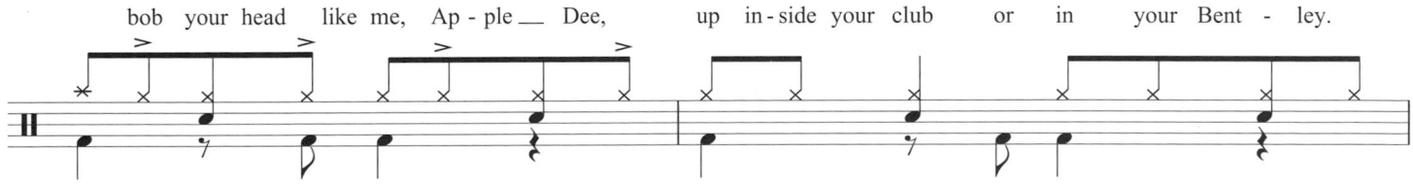
bob your head like me, Ap - ple Dee, up in - side your club or in your Bent - ley.

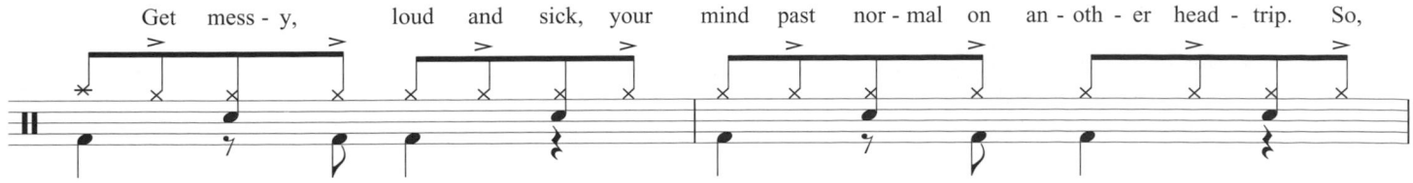
Get mess - y, loud and sick, your mind past nor - mal on an - oth - er head - trip. So,

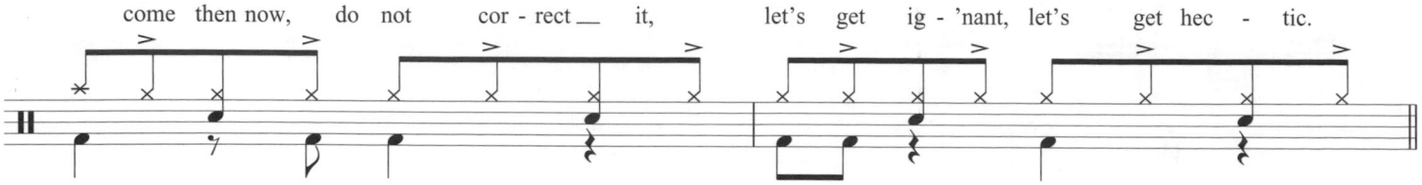

Pre-Chorus

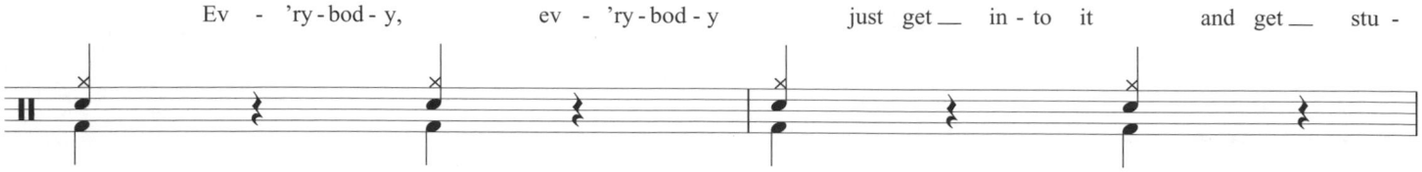

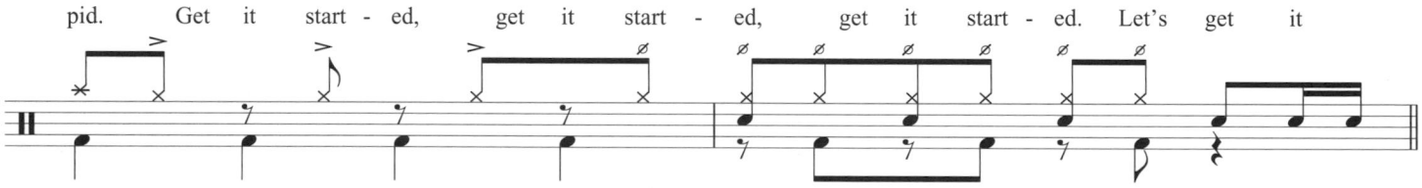

Chorus

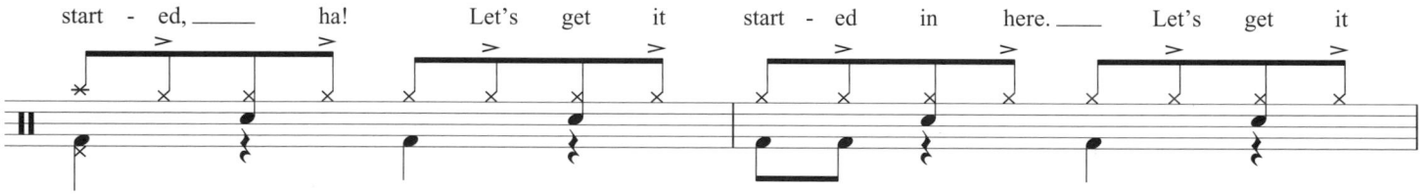

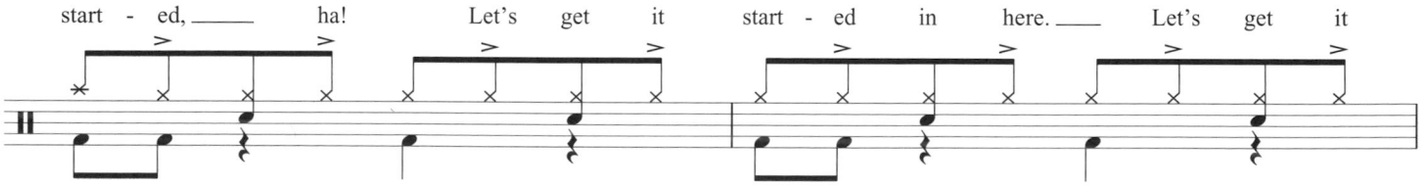

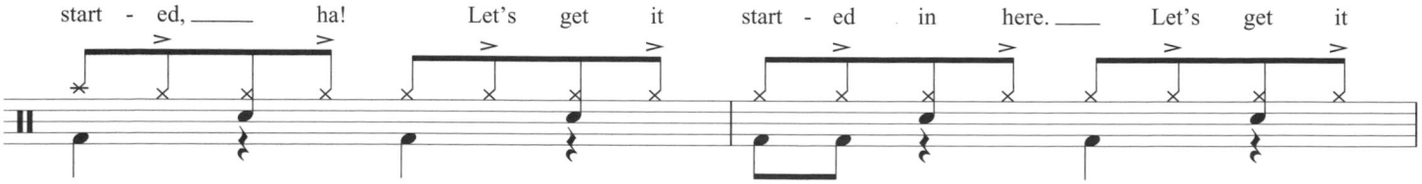

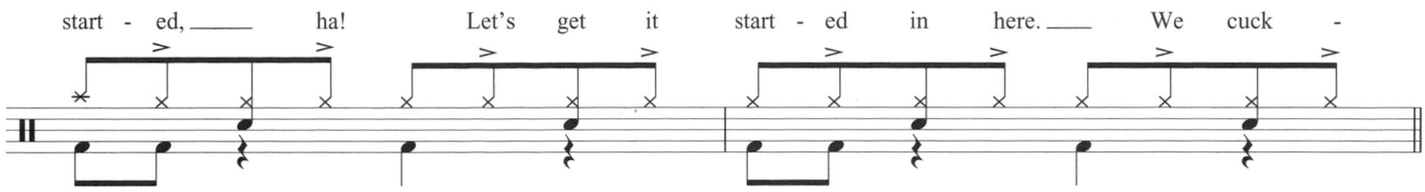

Outro

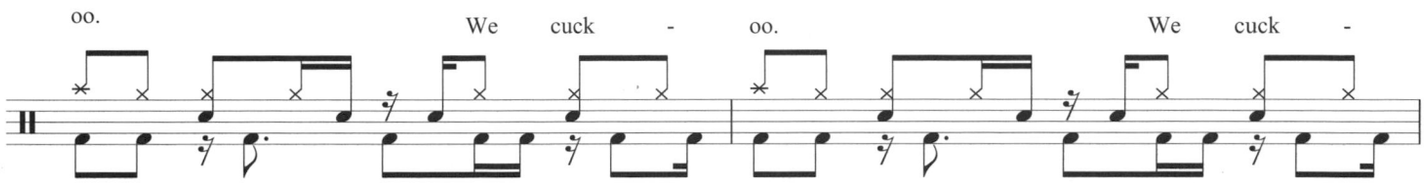

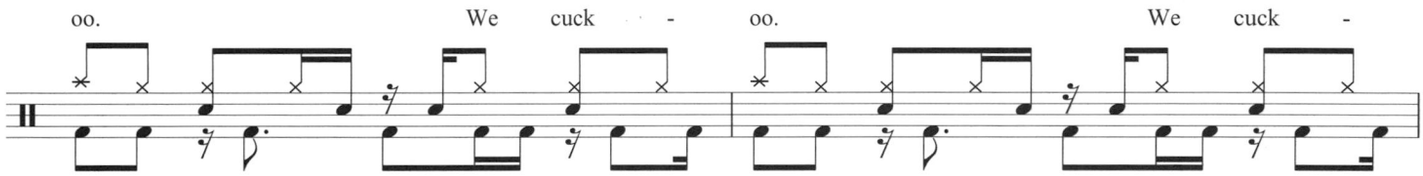

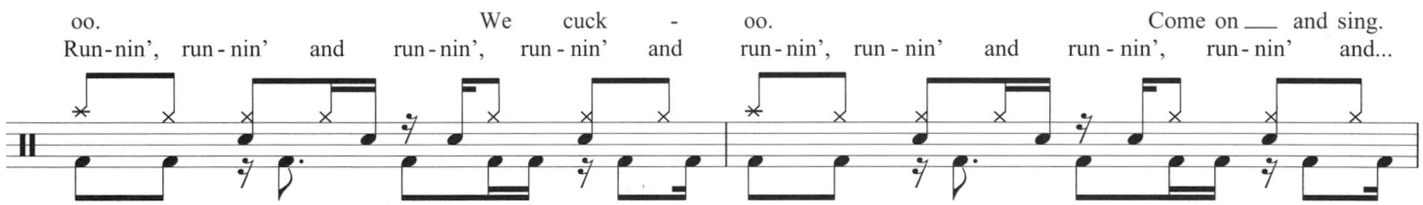

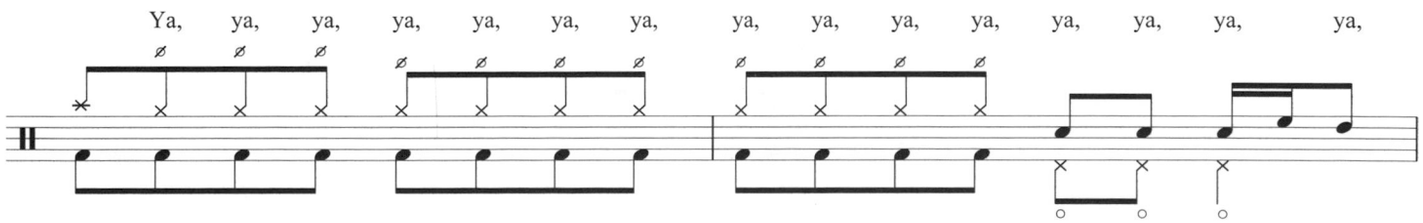

Repeat and fade

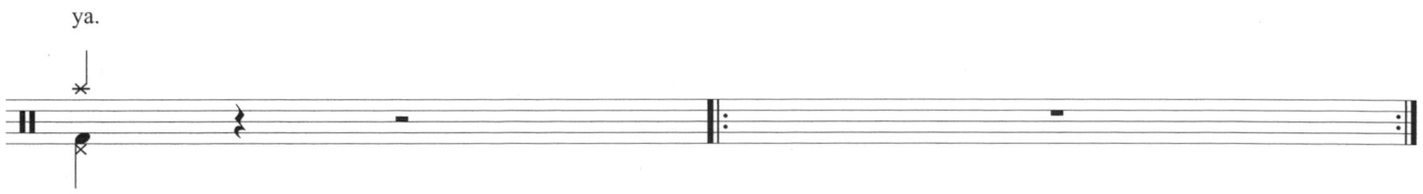

Surfin' U.S.A.

Words and Music by Chuck Berry

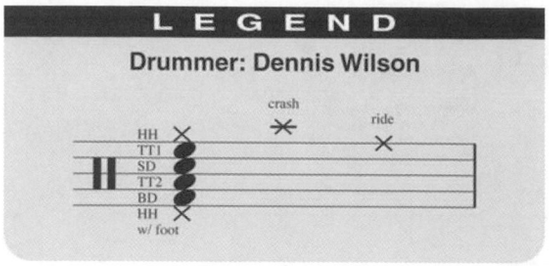

Intro

Moderately fast ♩ = 160

1. If ev - 'ry - bod - y had an

Verse

o - cean a - cross the U. S. A.,

2. *See additional lyrics*

then ev - 'ry - bod - y'd be surf - in' like Cal - i - forn - i - a.

You'd see 'em wear - ing their bag - gies,

Hua - ra - chi san - dals, too. A bush - y, bush - y blonde

hair - do, surf - in' U. S. A.

Copyright © 1958, 1963 (Renewed) by Arc Music Corp. (BMI) and Isalee Music Inc. (BMI)
Arc Music Corp. Administered by BMG Rights Management (US) LLC for the world excluding Japan and Southeast Asia
International Copyright Secured All Rights Reserved
Used by Permission

Chorus

2nd time, substitute Fill 1

You'll catch 'em surf - in' at Del Mar, Ven - tu - ra Coun - ty line.

See additional lyrics

San - ta Cruz and Trest - le,

Aus - tra - li - a's Nar - ra - been. All o - ver Man -

hat - tan and down Do - hen - y Way.

Ev - 'ry - bod - y's gone surf - in', surf - in' U. S. A.

1. 2.

2. We'll all be plan - nin' out a

Fill 1

Organ/Guitar Solo

Outro

Begin fade

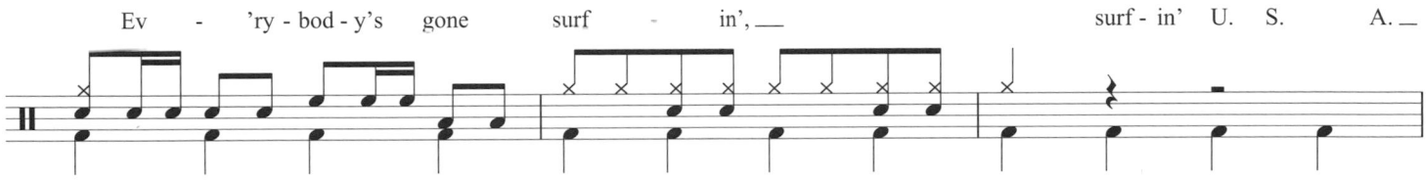

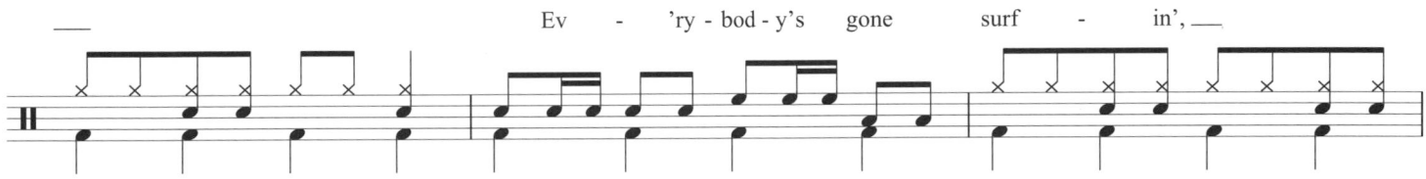

Fade out

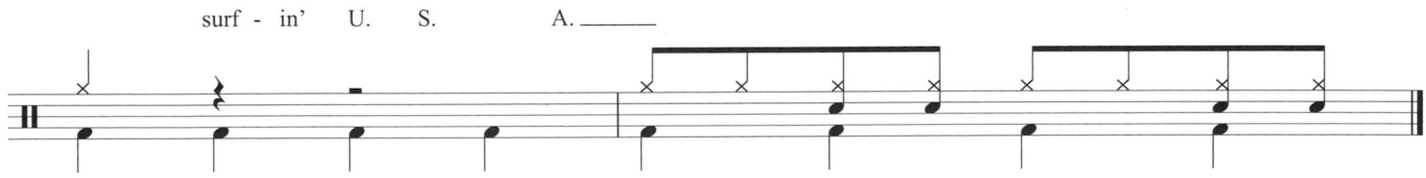

Additional Lyrics

2. We'll all be planning out a route we're gonna take real soon.
We're waxin' down our surfboards; we can't wait for June.
We'll all be gone for the summer; we're on safari to stay.
Tell the teacher we're surfin', surfin' U.S.A.

Chorus At Haggerty's and Swami's, Pacific Palisades.
San Onofre and Sunset, Redondo Beach, L.A.
All over La Jolla; at Waiamea Bay.
Ev'rybody's gone surfin', surfin' U.S.A.

Low Rider

Words and Music by Sylvester Allen, Harold R. Brown,
Morris Dickerson, Jerry Goldstein, Leroy Jordan,
Lee Oskar, Charles W. Miller and Howard Scott

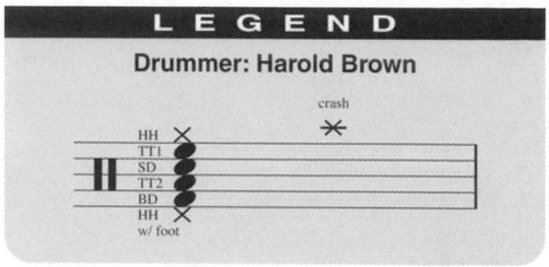

Intro

Moderately fast Rock ♩ = 138

Verse

1. All my friends know the low rid - er.

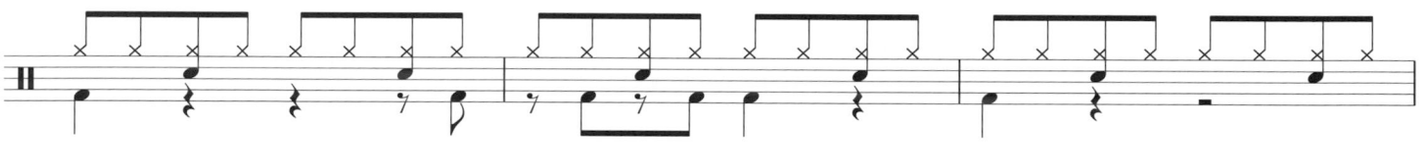

The low rid - er is a lit - tle

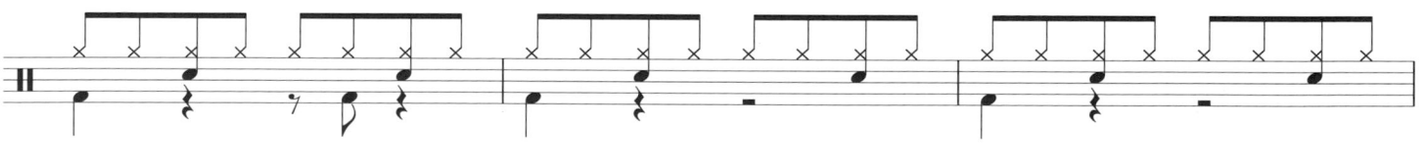

high - er.

Chorus

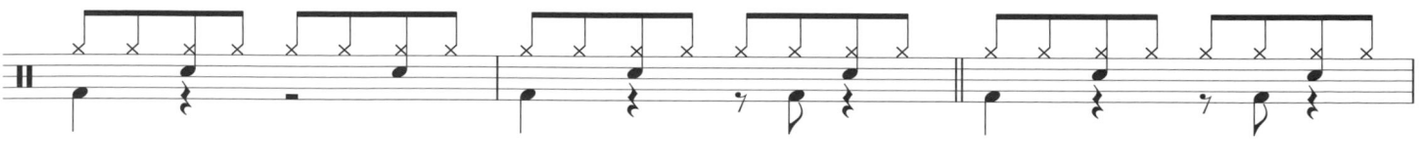

Copyright © 1975 Far Out Music, Inc.
Copyright Renewed
All Rights Administered by BMG Rights Management (US) LLC
All Rights Reserved Used by Permission

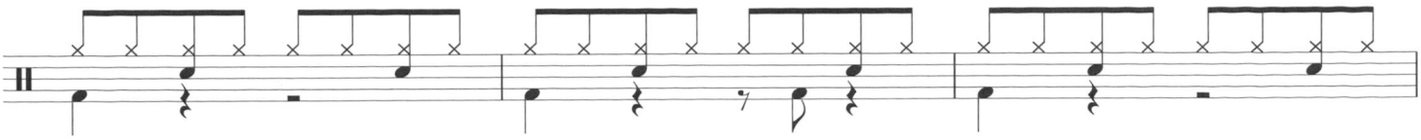

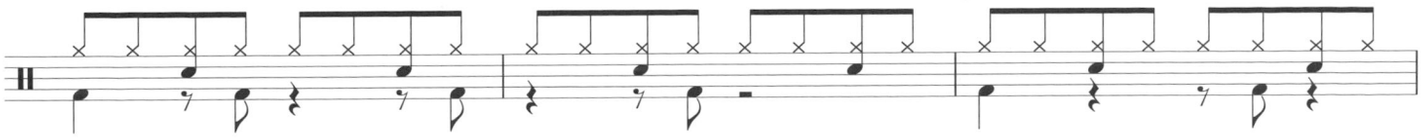

Verse

Chorus

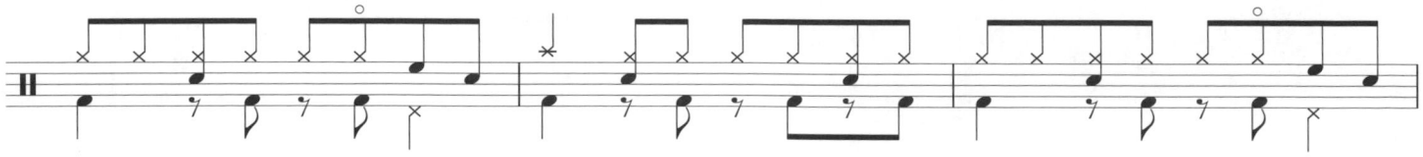

Verse

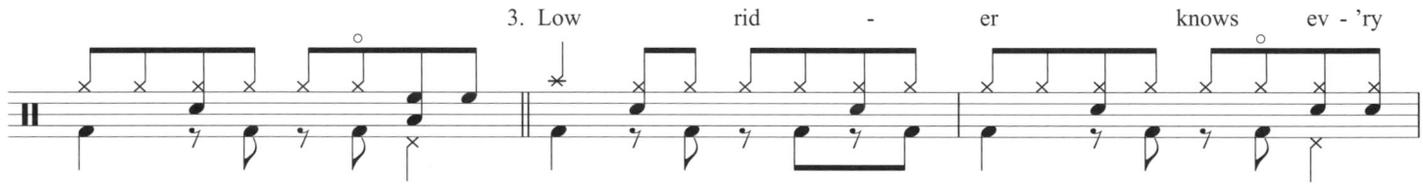

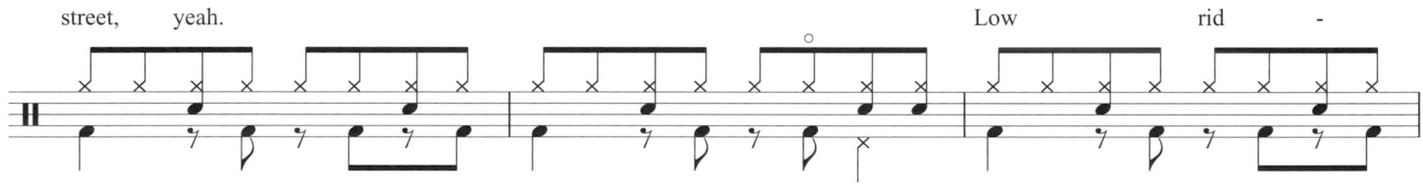

Chorus

Verse

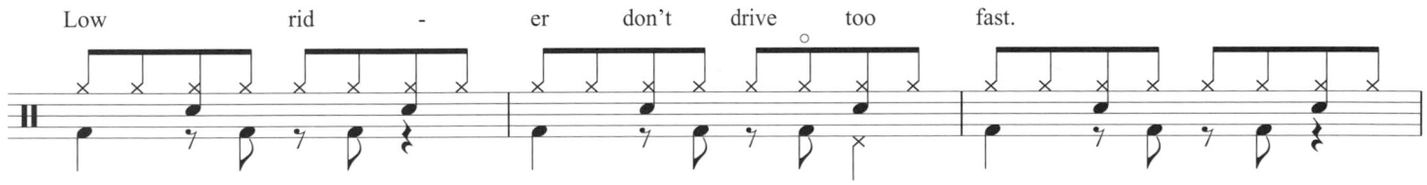

Chorus

Outro

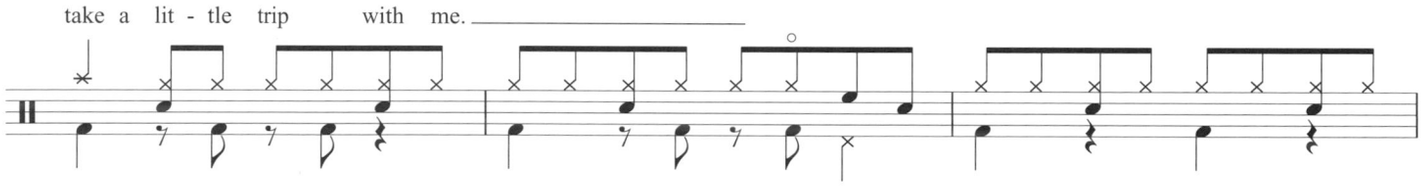

Repeat and fade

Yellow Submarine

Words and Music by John Lennon and Paul McCartney

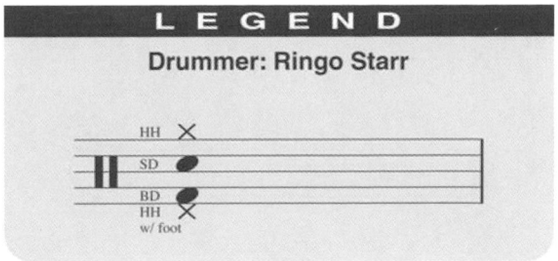

Verse

Moderately ♩ = 100 (♫ = ♩♪)

1. In the town _____ where I was born, lived a

man _____ who sail - ed to sea. And he told _

_____ us of his life ___ in the land _____ of sub - ma - rines. So we

sailed _____ on to the sun 'til we found _____ the sea of green. _ And we

lived be - neath the waves in our yel - low sub - ma - rine.

Chorus

We all live in a yel - low sub - ma - rine, yel - low sub - ma - rine,

Copyright © 1966 Sony/ATV Music Publishing LLC
Copyright Renewed
All Rights Administered by Sony/ATV Music Publishing LLC, 424 Church Street, Suite 1200, Nashville, TN 37219
International Copyright Secured All Rights Reserved

yel - low sub - ma - rine. We all live in a yel - low sub - ma - rine,
Verse
yel - low sub - ma - rine, yel - low sub - ma - rine. 2. And our friends _____ are all a -
board, man - y more of them live next door. And the
band _____ be - gins to ____ play.
Chorus
We all live in a yel - low sub - ma - rine, yel - low sub - ma - rine,
yel - low sub - ma - rine. We all live in a yel - low sub - ma - rine,
Interlude
yel - low sub - ma - rine, yel - low sub - ma - rine.

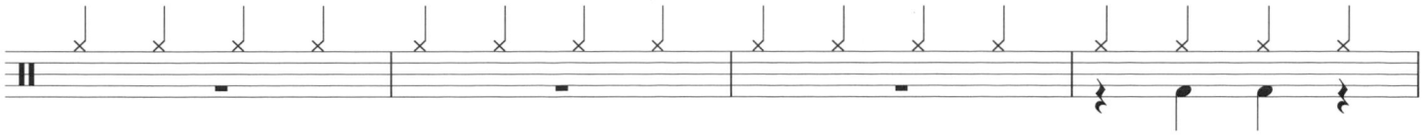

3. As we

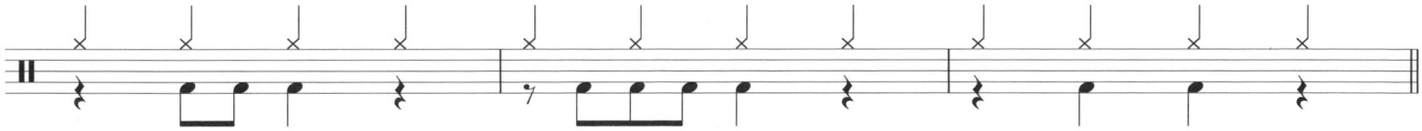

Verse

live a life of ease, ev - 'ry one of us has all we

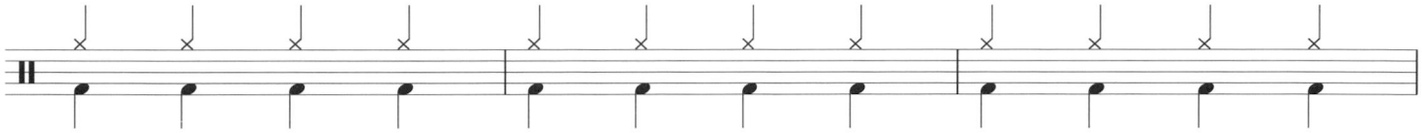

need. Sky of blue and sea of green, in our

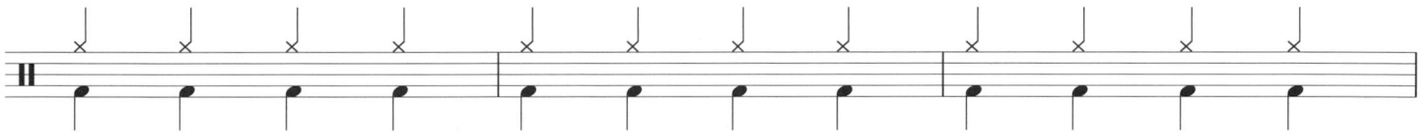

Outro-Chorus

yel - low sub - ma - rine. We all live in a

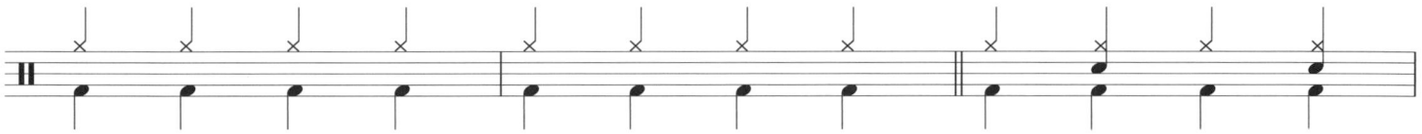

yel - low sub - ma - rine, a yel - low sub - ma - rine, yel - low sub - ma - rine.

We all live in a yel - low sub - ma - rine, a

Repeat and fade

yel - low sub - ma - rine, yel - low sub - ma - rine.

HAL•LEONARD®

DRUM PLAY-ALONG

AUDIO ACCESS INCLUDED

The Drum Play-Along™ Series will help you play your favorite songs quickly and easily! Just follow the drum notation, listen to the audio to hear how the drums should sound, and then play-along using the separate backing tracks. The lyrics are also included for reference. The audio files are enhanced so you can adjust the recording to any tempo without changing pitch!

1. Pop/Rock
00699742.....$14.99

2. Classic Rock
00699741.....$16.99

3. Hard Rock
00699743.....$17.99

4. Modern Rock
00699744.....$19.99

5. Funk
00699745.....$16.99

6. '90s Rock
00699746.....$17.99

7. Punk Rock
00699747.....$14.99

8. '80s Rock
00699832.....$16.99

9. Cover Band Hits
00211599.....$16.99

10. blink-182
00699834.....$19.99

11. Jimi Hendrix Experience: Smash Hits
00699835.....$19.99

12. The Police
00700268.....$16.99

13. Steely Dan
00700202.....$17.99

15. The Beatles
00256656.....$17.99

16. Blues
00700272.....$17.99

17. Nirvana
00700273.....$16.99

18. Motown
00700274.....$16.99

19. Rock Band: Modern Rock Edition
00700707.....$17.99

20. Rock Band: Classic Rock Edition
00700708.....$14.95

21. Weezer
00700959.....$14.99

22. Black Sabbath
00701190.....$17.99

23. The Who
00701191.....$19.99

24. Pink Floyd – Dark Side of the Moon
00701612.....$17.99

25. Bob Marley
00701703.....$19.99

26. Aerosmith
00701887.....$19.99

27. Modern Worship
00701921.....$16.99

28. Avenged Sevenfold
00702388.....$19.99

29. Queen
00702389.....$17.99

30. Dream Theater
00111942.....$24.99

31. Red Hot Chili Peppers
00702992.....$19.99

32. Songs for Beginners
00704204.....$15.99

33. James Brown
00117422.....$17.99

34. U2
00124470.....$17.99

35. Buddy Rich
00124640.....$19.99

36. Wipe Out & 7 Other Fun Songs
00125341.....$17.99

37. Slayer
00139861.....$17.99

38. Eagles
00143920.....$17.99

39. Kiss
00143937.....$16.99

40. Stevie Ray Vaughan
00146155.....$16.99

41. Rock Songs for Kids
00148113.....$15.99

42. Easy Rock Songs
00148143.....$15.99

45. Bon Jovi
00200891.....$17.99

46. Mötley Crüe
00200892.....$16.99

47. Metallica: 1983-1988
00234340.....$19.99

48. Metallica: 1991-2016
00234341.....$19.99

49. Top Rock Hits
00256655.....$16.99

51. Deep Purple
00278400.....$16.99

52. More Songs for Beginners
00278403.....$14.99

53. Pop Songs for Kids
00298650.....$15.99

HAL•LEONARD®

Visit Hal Leonard Online at
www.halleonard.com

Prices, contents and availability subject to change without notice and may vary outside the US.

0222
301